Goal-Setting to Support Cadet Success

Insights and Recommendations for the National
Guard Youth ChalleNGe Program

COLLEEN CORTE, LISA SONTAG-PADILLA

Prepared for the Office of the Secretary of Defense
Approved for public release; distribution unlimited

RAND NATIONAL DEFENSE RESEARCH INSTITUTE

For more information on this publication, visit **www.rand.org/t/RRA271-6**.

About RAND

The RAND Corporation is a research organization that develops solutions to public policy challenges to help make communities throughout the world safer and more secure, healthier and more prosperous. RAND is nonprofit, nonpartisan, and committed to the public interest. To learn more about RAND, visit www.rand.org.

Research Integrity

Our mission to help improve policy and decisionmaking through research and analysis is enabled through our core values of quality and objectivity and our unwavering commitment to the highest level of integrity and ethical behavior. To help ensure our research and analysis are rigorous, objective, and nonpartisan, we subject our research publications to a robust and exacting quality-assurance process; avoid both the appearance and reality of financial and other conflicts of interest through staff training, project screening, and a policy of mandatory disclosure; and pursue transparency in our research engagements through our commitment to the open publication of our research findings and recommendations, disclosure of the source of funding of published research, and policies to ensure intellectual independence. For more information, visit www.rand.org/about/principles.

RAND's publications do not necessarily reflect the opinions of its research clients and sponsors.

Published by the RAND Corporation, Santa Monica, Calif.
© 2021 RAND Corporation
RAND® is a registered trademark.

Library of Congress Cataloging-in-Publication Data is available for this publication.
ISBN: 978-1-9774-0784-9

About This Report

The National Guard Youth Challenge (ChalleNGe) Program is a residential, quasi-military program for youth ages 16 to 18 who are experiencing difficulty in traditional high school. Established in 1993, the program, which has 40 sites across the United States, is a community-based program that leads, trains, and mentors youth so that they may become productive citizens. The Post-Residential Action Plan (P-RAP) is a process used by ChalleNGe to assist at-risk youth with identifying placement goals for the post-residential phase and developing a plan to achieve these goals. The implementation and utility of the P-RAP process across sites has not been examined. The purpose of this project was to examine the various approaches to using P-RAP across ChalleNGe sites, draw insights from the literature on best or promising practices for goal-setting in adolescence, and provide recommendations on the use of the P-RAP in the ChalleNGe Program.

This report will be of interest to ChalleNGe Program staff and to personnel providing oversight for the program, and more broadly, to practitioners, educators, and policymakers concerned with designing effective programs for at-risk youth.

RAND National Security Research Division

The research reported here was completed in June 2021 and underwent security review with the sponsor and the Defense Office of Prepublication and Security Review before public release.

This research was sponsored by the Office of the Assistant Secretary of Defense for Manpower and Reserve Affairs and conducted within the Forces and Resources Policy Center of the RAND National Security Research Division (NSRD), which operates the National Defense Research Institute (NDRI), a federally funded research and development center sponsored by the Office of the Secretary of Defense, the Joint Staff, the Unified Combatant Commands, the Navy, the Marine Corps, the defense agencies, and the defense intelligence enterprise.

Key Findings

In line with the literature highlighting the importance of goal-setting to help adolescents—particularly those at risk for academic, social, or behavioral problems—and to establish a pathway to independence and success in adulthood, the P-RAP process offers a way to support cadets in the identification and attainment of placement goals. Many aspects of the P-RAP process are well-grounded in goal-setting and adolescent development theory. There is empirical evidence that the process is well-designed to assist youth in identifying highly personalized goals and developing action-oriented plans to assist young people in achieving their goals and successfully transitioning to adult roles.

However, there is considerable variation in implementation of the P-RAP process across sites. Indeed, some sites appear to follow the promising practices set out in the literature, such as ensuring adequate exploration of potential goals and formulating goals that are both specific and attainable. Other sites appear to view the P-RAP process as less central to eventual success. Fortunately, the literature on goal-setting offers specific findings and recommendations that can assist ChalleNGe sites to further integrate the P-RAP process into their overall program.

Recommendations

Recognizing the need to allow for flexibility in the implementation of the P-RAP process across sites because of staff capacity and cadet needs, we recommend a small number of fundamental practices that should be followed with as much consistency as possible: (1) encourage deep and consistent use of the P-RAP across the components of ChalleNGe, (2) ensure adequate exploration and experiences to help cadets identify meaningful goals, (3) help cadets outline goals that are specific, challenging, and attainable, and (4) incorporate goals that are oriented toward learning specific skills. Moving toward a more standardized approach to the P-RAP process has the potential to strengthen the program and thus better prepare participants for long-term success.

Contents

APPENDIXES

CHAPTER ONE

Introduction

Background

Goal-setting, or the process of establishing clear and usable targets for learning, is linked to academic achievement; prosocial behaviors and fewer behavioral problems; and workforce readiness (e.g., Bruhn et al., 2016; Moeller, Theiler, and Wu, 2012; Schippers, Scheepers, and Peterson, 2015; Clements and Kamau, 2018). In turn, goal-setting is a process central to youths' successful transition from adolescence to adulthood. For many young people, goal-setting is a normal part of development, and they receive considerable support and guidance from parents, high school counselors, and teachers regarding education and career-related goals. But for economically disadvantaged youth, goal-setting might be more challenging for a variety of reasons (e.g., chronic stress within the home or community, fewer models of success in the social environment, limited availability for key adults to provide support) (Evans and Kim, 2013; Phillips and Pittman, 2003). Although a multitude of factors affect academic and career success, youth who struggle with setting goals might be more likely to demonstrate poorer academic performance, struggle with high school completion, and experience under- or unemployment (Engle and Black, 2008; Farley and Kim-Spoon, 2018).

The National Guard Youth Challenge (ChalleNGe) Program is a quasi-military program for at-risk youth ages 16 to 18 who either have dropped out or are at risk of dropping out of school; many are also exhibiting behavioral problems (Constant et al., 2019). The program consists of a 5.5-month residential phase followed by a 12-month post-residential phase. During the 5.5-month residential phase, cadets are fully immersed in a military-type training environment. The program emphasizes structured classroom work, discipline, and consistency with a focus on developing social, emotional, academic, and basic life skills. This is accomplished through the implementation of the eight core components (academic excellence, health and hygiene, job skills, leadership and followership, life-coping skills, physical fitness, responsible citizenship, and service to community). Cadets complete the residential phase with the skills and values necessary for their successful transition and integration into adult society. Following the residential phase, cadets transition to the 12-month post-residential phase where they leave the academy and return to their communities. After completing ChalleNGe, graduates may return to high school, pursue higher education, find a job, or join the military; taking part in any combination of these for at least 25 hours per week is referred to as a *placement*. Some graduates pursue volunteer opportunities in their home communities while searching for other opportunities. The goal of this phase is for graduates to sustain and build on the gains made during the residential phase, and to apply the new skills they have learned to their home environment. In addition, they must continue to develop and implement their life plans.

One of the key processes of the ChalleNGe Program is goal-setting. To support goal-setting, all ChalleNGe Programs use a process called the Post-Residential Action Plan (or P-RAP). Although implementation of the P-RAP varies across different ChalleNGe sites, broadly this process involves cadets documenting their short-, medium-, and long-term career goals, and delineating the steps required to meet these goals (Appendix A contains an example of a P-RAP template from the Wisconsin program). Based on the existing literature around goal-setting, the P-RAP process has great potential to positively influence ChalleNGe cadets' trajectories following participation in the program. Yet, little has been documented regarding the implementation of and experiences with the P-RAP process.

Aims of This Report

The objective of this report is to examine the various approaches to using the P-RAP across ChalleNGe sites, identify key challenges to implementing the P-RAP, and draw insights from the literature on best practices for implementing goal-setting strategies in adolescents. This report is intended to inform and further bolster the ChalleNGe Programs' efforts to maximize the effectiveness of the P-RAP across sites.

2

Approach

We used three main methods to achieve our aims: literature review, examination of P-RAP documents, and review of data on implementation approaches for the P-RAP. Here, we describe each of these approaches.

Literature Review

To help identify insights from the literature on the factors integral to goal-setting and the successful transition to adulthood in adolescents, we engaged in a narrative literature review focusing heavily on the role of goal-setting in adolescent success (academics, behavior, and employment), as well as contextual factors that affect the potential success of goal-setting behaviors. To carry out the literature review, we conducted a narrative review, including targeted keyword searches (e.g., goal-setting, identity development, possible selves, self-concept, adolescent/adolescence, youth, academic, career, and at-risk) of the PsycInfo, PubMed, and Google Scholar databases, focusing on meta-analyses and systematic literature reviews from 2010 and onward. Starting with this literature, we then reviewed the reference sections to capture any additional seminal studies originally missed by our searches. Given the history of work in the area of goal-setting, we included seminal research studies from dates prior to 2010. Findings from our review are highlighted in Chapter Two.

We categorized the findings under three topic areas: (1) role of the self-concept in behavioral self-regulation, (2) role of the self-concept in goal-setting, and (3) role of the self-concept in identity development.

Examination of P-RAP Templates from Select ChalleNGe Sites

Second, we examined P-RAP templates across 15 ChalleNGe sites. We requested that sites provide a blank copy of their P-RAP template as part of the RAND Corporation's site visits in 2017–2018. We received P-RAP templates from 11 sites (Hawaii, Idaho, Indiana, Kentucky, Montana, New Jersey, New Mexico, Oregon, Virginia, West Virginia, and Wyoming) via email in October 2018. We obtained an additional four P-RAP templates during visits to four sites (California, Illinois, Michigan, and Wisconsin). These 15 sites represent about 40 percent of all ChalleNGe sites. Given the size of the sample, the results that describe variation in P-RAP templates and the process to using them might not capture all of the variation in the P-RAP process across all sites, although we believe that the overall findings from the literature apply to all sites. Appendix A contains a sample P-RAP template.

Meetings with Select ChalleNGe Sites About Current P-RAP Practices

Third, we drew information on implementation approaches from summary data collected from approximately 30 site visits in 2017–2018 and from additional, focused site visits to discuss the P-RAP with ChalleNGe staff at four sites (Wisconsin, December 2018; Michigan, December 2018; California, September 2019; and Illinois, March 2018).[1] In our visits to ChalleNGe sites, we focused on how the sites use the P-RAP and the extent to which approaches to implementation of the P-RAP vary. The 30 initial site visits generally included discussions with eight to ten individual staff members. The protocol included a few questions about how the sites used the P-RAP and the extent to which sites found the document helpful; researchers recorded responses to these questions for each site. Researchers also collected examples of the P-RAP from programs; this allowed the research team to see how the form had been modified at each site. The four additional, focused site visits included more-detailed discussions of how the sites used or implemented the P-RAP and the extent to which the P-RAP was integrated into their broader curriculum. The information from the site visits was analyzed with a goal of identifying broad themes that appeared at multiple sites. Because of the quasi-structured nature of the protocol and the relatively small number of observations, the information from the site visits was not analyzed with a more systematic process to identifying qualitative themes (e.g., using analytic software, such as InVivo). Appendix B includes relevant information from the protocols.

---

[1] These site visits were carried out as part of a larger project. Before beginning our work, we applied for and received appropriate permissions from RAND's Human Subjects Protection Committee; we also applied for and received concurrence from the Department of Defense's review system. RAND's Human Subjects Protection Committee determined that the discussions with program staff were properly categorized as "not research."

CHAPTER TWO

Goal-Setting During Adolescence: Insights from the Literature

The successful transition to adulthood is contingent on an individual's ability to regulate their behavior and set meaningful goals. Broadly, goal-setting is the process of establishing clear and usable targets, or objectives, for learning. Although goal-setting is applicable well beyond the period of adolescence (e.g., much of the goal-setting literature focuses on adulthood and organizational and workforce success; Latham and Locke, 2007; Seijts and Latham, 2011), the aim of this chapter is to highlight the centrality of goal-setting to the developmental tasks of adolescence. In this chapter, we describe the results of our literature review, which focused on the factors integral to goal-setting and the successful transition from adolescence to adulthood. The results are organized into three sections, which focus on the role of goal-setting during adolescence, characteristics of effective goal-setting, and supports and strategies to promote goal-setting in adolescence.

Goal-Setting and Self-Concept During Adolescence

The transition from adolescence to adulthood is fraught with challenges as young people strive to determine who they are and who they want to be. Identity development is one of the major life tasks of adolescence (Erikson, 1968), and key developmental milestones include important decisions about education, employment, residential independence, and intimate relationships. During the process of identity development, adolescents explore options and make commitments (or set goals) in a variety of life domains, such as vocation, religion, relational choices, gender roles, and so on. Ideally, adolescents explore various opportunities prior to making commitments, e.g., to a career, life partner, etc. Compared with adolescents from greater socioeconomic advantage, adolescents from lower socioeconomic backgrounds typically engage in lower levels of exploration, perhaps because of fewer opportunities to explore and the internalization of negative messages about their potential from the social environment (Phillips and Pittman, 2003). For instance, a study of racially and ethnically diverse eighth graders showed that economic hardship (i.e., the degree to which parents had difficulty paying bills and meeting basic needs) was negatively associated with adolescents' commitment to a variety of normative goals related to family, friends, career, being a student, ethnicity, and religion (De Haan and MacDermid, 1999). In addition to limited opportunities for exploration (Phillips and Pittman, 2003), youth from economically disadvantaged backgrounds might have fewer positive identities (e.g., friend, good son) and a higher number of negative identities influenced by social stigmas (e.g., bad student, thug) (Hihara, Sugimura, and Syed, 2018). This is important because positive identities are associated with positive mood and adaptive behavioral outcomes, whereas negative identities are associated with negative mood and maladaptive behavioral outcomes (Corte and Zucker, 2008; Flouri and Panourgia, 2014; Gong, Chen, and Lee, 2020), which in turn increase risk for academic and social challenges for youth.

Given the relatively poor experiences many cadets had in their previous high schools and the disadvantaged neighborhoods in which many of them lived (Wenger et al., forthcoming), risk for having few positive and many negative identities might be an obstacle for many youth in the ChalleNGe Program to overcome. Together, these findings underscore the importance of helping adolescents—particularly at-risk youth, such as those in the ChalleNGe Program—establish and explore career and educational opportunities and develop clear goals with a plan to pursue them during this pivotal developmental period of adolescence.

Goal-Setting and Success

In addition to being a central developmental task of identity formation, the process of goal-setting can positively affect students' academic, social, and career-related trajectories. Indeed, studies have shown that by helping students develop clear and concise targets and asking students to generate and reflect on their goals, students are more likely to demonstrate academic success as early as elementary school up through postsecondary education. For instance, based on a longitudinal study of 1,273 students in 21 classrooms using a Spanish-as-a-second-language program focused on student self-assessment and goal-setting, researchers found students with greater goal-setting practices (goal, action plan, or reflection scores) were more likely to demonstrate higher Spanish proficiency scores in reading, writing, or speaking (Moeller, Theiler, and Wu, 2012). In a quasi-experimental study of first-year college students participating in a brief, online intervention aimed at enhancing goal-directed conceptualization (703 students in intervention; 896, 825, and 720 in a wait-listed group), researchers found support for the link between goal-setting and academic achievement (Schippers, Scheepers, and Peterson, 2015). Based on goal-setting theory (Austin and Vancouver, 1996; Locke and Latham, 2002; Locke et al., 1994; Duckworth et al., 2013; Schunk, 1990), the intervention was designed to help students produce clear and specific goals, instead of more-general *do your best* goals, to avoid potential goal conflicts, and to encourage them to assess whether their goals were practical and attainable. Additionally, the intervention required students to make a mental comparison of the future and the present and to develop *if-then* strategies for dealing with potential obstacles as a way to form plans for assessing and monitoring progress toward their goals. Results demonstrated that all groups (male vs. female, ethnic minority vs. majority) in the intervention cohort performed significantly better than control cohorts. The increase in performance was largest for ethnic minority males, who earned 44 percent more credits and demonstrated a 54 percent increase in retention rate (Schippers, Scheepers, and Peterson, 2015). These findings may be particularly relevant to the ChalleNGe Program because these demographics reflect a large percentage of the program's cadets.

In addition to academic performance, research suggests a link between goal-setting and behavioral outcomes in youth. Youth at risk for social and behavioral problems often struggle with self-regulation (i.e., the ability to control one's behavior, emotions, and thoughts in the pursuit of long-term goals), which in turn might affect their ability to appropriately engage with others and achieve academic success. To improve self-regulation skills, students at risk for such behavioral problems might benefit from being taught explicit self-regulation strategies such as goal-setting. Although goal-setting has focused mostly on academic and life skills, behavioral goal-setting has demonstrated promise as a strategy for establishing healthy developmental pathways for at-risk youth (Bruhn et al., 2016). Based on a systematic review of 39 peer-reviewed studies, researchers found goal-setting to be a useful strategy in helping at-risk youth improve behavioral outcomes (Bruhn et al., 2016). Additionally, students were more likely to attain their goals when they were involved directly in setting those goals (Barbrack and Maher, 1984; Hill and Brown, 2013; Maher, 1981). These findings, consistent with goal-setting theory, emphasize the idea that when goals are self-set, people are more likely to commit to attaining those goals (Locke and Latham, 2002). Although most studies identified in the review focused on elementary populations (Bruhn et al., 2016), the utility of goal-setting for adolescents more broadly still holds appeal for youth who have struggled with self-regulation challenges, as may be the case for many incoming ChalleNGe cadets.

Although there have been hundreds of studies supporting the goal-setting framework (Latham and Locke, 2007; Seijts and Latham, 2011), few studies have evaluated its applicability to career-related outcomes in older adolescents or emerging adults. That said, recent studies demonstrate promise for goal-setting related to postsecondary and career-related outcomes. One recent study of 432 undergraduate students from 21 United Kingdom universities found that students who reported higher levels of mastery approach (i.e., they focused on skill development or self-improvement) were more likely to perceive themselves as employable post university compared with students who engaged in lower levels of mastery approach (Clements and Kamau, 2018). Additionally, students' career goal commitment was positively associated with all four proactive career behaviors (career planning, skill development, career consultation, and network building) (Clements and Kamau, 2018). Although reliant on self-reported behaviors and perceived employability, this study suggests the potential positive impact of goal-setting on pursuing and attaining suitable career pathways following high school and postsecondary education.

Characteristics of Effective Goal-Setting

Although research such as the studies outlined previously demonstrates a clear link between goal-setting and academic, behavioral, and career-related outcomes, goal-setting theory and its supporting literature demonstrate that the positive outcomes can vary significantly based on the quality and characteristics of the goal-setting process. Next, we outline some of the most-frequently cited characteristics of goal-setting associated with successful goal attainment or academic success.

Learning-Oriented Goals

Goal-setting theory (Locke and Latham, 1990, 2002) proposes that there are two general goal orientations students can adopt: learning goals with an *intrinsic* focus on increasing one's competency, understanding, and appreciation for what is being learned versus performance goals with an *extrinsic* focus on external rewards and outperforming others (e.g., getting good grades and doing better than other students) (Dweck, 1986; Dweck and Leggett, 1988; Elliott and Dweck, 1988). Learning-oriented students tend to believe that their effort is the key to their success and that their failure does not necessarily suggest that they are incompetent, but simply that they have not used the right approach or might need to spend more time improving their skill (Nicholls, 1984; Pintrich and Schunk, 1996). In contrast, performance-oriented students are driven by fears of incompetency, with some striving to avoid failure by succeeding (approach style) and the others setting up failures when necessary, but in ways that deflect the implication that they are incompetent (avoidance style). Extensive research on learning versus performance goals demonstrates a consistent positive link between learning-goal orientation and various precursors and markers of academic success, such as academic self-efficacy (Coutinho and Neuman, 2008; Phan, 2009), self-regulation (Hsieh et al., 2012), and academic achievement (Crippen et al., 2009; Hsieh, Sullivan, and Guerra, 2007; Phan, 2009).

Personally Meaningful Goals

Identifying personally meaningful goals is an important part of the goal-setting process, and in turn a potentially important part of the successful transition to adulthood. Future-oriented identities, called "possible identities," are *personally meaningful* goals. They represent the selves one hopes to be (hoped-for identities), expects to be (expected identities), and fears becoming (feared identities) (Lee et al., 2015; Markus and Nurius, 1986; Stein, Roeser, and Markus, 1998). Possible identities are a bridge between the present and the future, and they serve as the link between motivation and behavior (Markus and Nurius, 1986; Nurra and Oyserman, 2018). They facilitate optimism and foster a belief that change is possible because they provide a sense that the current self is changeable (Markus and Nurius, 1986). In short, possible identities serve as the framework for motivating and regulating behavior toward the achievement of the end goal and as behavioral standards for evaluating the current self and one's patterns of behavior (Hoyle and Sherrill, 2006).

Evidence from studies of college students and adults suggests that episodic future thinking (imagining future-oriented goals) might facilitate the transformation of the goal into an enduring belief about the self. In one study, college students were asked to imagine themselves as a person who exercises regularly (hoped-for possible identity) or fails to exercise regularly (feared possible identity), and then asked them to complete writing tasks about these possible identity images (Ouellette et al., 2005). In another study, participants were asked to imagine themselves in the future as either healthy, regular exercisers or as unhealthy, inactive individuals (Murru and Martin Ginis, 2010). And in a third study, inactive adults were asked to imagine themselves in the future as physically active (Strachan et al., 2017). In all cases, the possible identity intervention groups had better outcomes than the control groups, suggesting that episodic future thinking might motivate behavior change and facilitate goal attainment.

Specific, Challenging, and Attainable Goals

In addition to being personally meaningful, possible identities or future-oriented goals must also be specific, challenging, and perceived as attainable (Locke and Latham, 1990, 2002, 2006; Zhu et al., 2014). According to goal-setting theory (Locke and Latham, 1990, 2002, 2006)—which was established over decades of work and has been supported by hundreds of research studies—specific, challenging goals stimulate goal-directed behavior and boost performance more than easy goals or vague, abstract goals such as "do your best." For instance, career goals that are clear and specific (e.g., I hope/expect to get a job as an electrician) are more motivating than goals that

are more general (e.g., I hope/expect to be successful). Creating specific time bounds is also helpful in assisting adolescents with establishing specific and attainable goals. For instance, there is evidence that fine-grained time metrics (365 days versus one year) create a sense that the future and present selves are connected, potentially creating concrete connections between actions done now and outcomes in the near future (Lewis and Oyserman, 2015). This framework underlies the SMART (specific, measurable, attainable, realistic, time-bound) goals approach widely used in postsecondary counseling and the corporate world.[1] The literature also indicates that explicit goals are more likely to be met (Nurra and Oyserman, 2018). However, to date, research examining the use of SMART goals with adolescents is limited. One recent study of 80 emergency medicine residents at three academic hospitals compared the effectiveness of SMART-goal-enhanced debriefing after clinic with a standard debriefing. Residents who used the SMART goals executed more educational actions than those using the standard debriefing. However, the number and quality of learning goals reported by residents were not improved (Aghera et al., 2017). Although the evidence base is sparse, high school and college counselors anecdotally find great utility in SMART goals as a way to offer structure to the goal-setting process (college counselor, verbal discussion with the authors, February 2021).[2]

Together, these frameworks and findings suggest the benefit of helping ChalleNGe cadets develop and foster learning-oriented goals that focus on improving one's skills and mastery of a task, identifying personally meaningful goals, and developing a plan to achieve these goals that is specific and challenging yet also attainable based on cadets' personal abilities.

Supports and Strategies to Promote Successful Goal-Setting and Attainment

Although few evidence-based practices for goal-setting during adolescence exist, there are some programs that have demonstrated promising results

---

[1] Considerable evidence suggests that effective goals can be described by the acronym SMART (Drucker, 1954).

[2] Throughout the report, additional details about interpersonal communications are withheld to protect participants' confidentiality.

in fostering successful goal-setting and attainment for youth. A pertinent example is Check-In/Check-Out (CICO), a commonly used approach to help youth at risk for social, emotional, and behavioral problems by providing daily support in managing their behavior and ultimately reducing behavioral problems, increasing academic engagement, and reducing referrals for more-intensive behavioral interventions (Hawken et al., 2014; Mitchell, Adamson, and McKenna, 2017). In CICO, students check in with an adult (typically guidance counselors or teachers) at the beginning of each day to be sure they are prepared for class and ready to learn. Throughout the day, students check in with teachers and receive points on a card (0, 1, or 2) related to how closely they met school-wide behavior expectations. At the end of the day, students check out with an adult who totals up the points. If it's part of the routine, students take their point cards home to share with their parents and the card gets turned in the next morning at check-in. This cycle repeats itself each day. Although this process focused on changing behavioral patterns, the regular involvement of adults and the students in setting their goals might be relevant practices for the ChalleNGe Program to consider. The potential importance of adult mentors is underscored by the plethora of research that finds mentoring is associated with a wide variety of favorable behavioral, attitudinal, health-related, relational, motivational, and career outcomes for youth and adults alike, although the effect size is generally small (Eby et al., 2008).

Of particular relevance to the ChalleNGe Program and the P-RAPs, interventions to foster the development of possible identities have been shown to effectively change behavior. These interventions have been developed and tested in youth as young as middle school. For example, Oyserman, Terry, and Bybee, 2002, developed a "School-to-Jobs" intervention for inner-city African American eighth graders. The intervention was composed of activities designed to foster the ability of youth to imagine themselves as "successful adults" and connect those possible identities to current school involvement. At the end of the school year, youth in the intervention group had greater bonding to school, more concern about doing well in school, and better school attendance than youth in the control group. Another study found that seventh-graders who participated in an occupation-related possible identity intervention were less likely to engage in risky behavior 19 weeks after baseline than students in the control group (Clark et al., 2005).

Key Takeaways

Goal-setting has been shown to facilitate pathways of success during adolescence and beyond. Specifically, research suggests goal-setting can positively affect students' academic, social, and career-related trajectories.

But certain types of goals are much more likely to be associated with positive outcomes. Specifically, learning-oriented goals that focus on improving one's skills and mastery of a task, personally meaningful goals, and goals that are specific and challenging yet also attainable based on one's abilities (SMART goals) are associated with greater attainment of goals and ultimately success in areas relevant to the transition from adolescence to adulthood.

Interventions that integrate goal-setting (e.g., CICO) and foster the development of possible identities have been shown to effectively change behavior. These programs include elements supported in the literature, such as a focus on future-oriented goals and exploration of possible selves; regular check-ins with adults that provide opportunities for reflection and input from youth; opportunities for positive reinforcement from adults (e.g., school-based staff); and the utilization of more–fine-grained time metrics when defining goals.

To summarize, the goal-setting literature contains several implications for the ChalleNGe Program. First, among adolescents, goal-setting is associated with success across multiple areas—including school and work, but also in social and behavioral arenas. The importance of goal-setting, coupled with the finding that young people from disadvantaged backgrounds typically lack some of the resources required for successful goal-setting, suggest that the ChalleNGe Program's focus on goals and use of the P-RAP process are completely appropriate. The literature also suggests that goals that can be described as specific, meaningful, appropriate, and learning-oriented are especially likely to be associated with positive outcomes. Finally, the literature indicates that certain interventions should be a part of goal-setting. A specific example is CICO, but more generally the literature shows that the regular and positive intervention of adults is associated with positive outcomes.

In the next chapter, we examine the specific ways in which the different ChalleNGe sites approach the P-RAP process; in the final chapter, we combine findings from the literature with the ChalleNGe site's practices to develop a series of recommendations.

CHAPTER THREE

Conceptualization and Implementation of the P-RAP

To gain an understanding of the integration of the P-RAP process in the overall ChalleNGe Program and describe the similarities and differences in the implementation process across sites, we engaged in two strategies. First, we reviewed templates from 15 sites (California, Hawaii, Idaho, Illinois, Indiana, Kentucky, Michigan, Montana, New Jersey, New Mexico, Oregon, Virginia, West Virginia, Wisconsin, and Wyoming) that implement the P-RAP process. We reviewed the overall format of the P-RAP templates and looked for characteristics and processes known to be associated with effective goal-setting (e.g., using SMART goals; the use of time horizons for short-term, intermediate, and future-oriented long-term goals; and whether the template outlined steps for achieving goals, such as developing *if-then* strategies to deal with obstacles).

Second, of the 15 sites that provided templates, we examined notes from previous site visits at 11 of the sites and conducted P-RAP-focused site visits with four locations (California, Illinois, Michigan, and Wisconsin). The notes from previous site visits included short conversations about the P-RAP; the P-RAP-focused visits used a semi-structured protocol that included more-extensive questions about the programs' perceptions of the utility of the P-RAP, how staff use the P-RAP process, and other aspects of the process implementation. Information from the protocols used appears in Appendix B.

Next, we synthesize our findings from both approaches to describe the implementation of the P-RAP process overall and also around key themes that emerged from our synthesis.

Overview of Implementation

The P-RAP process is used within the ChalleNGe Program to assist cadets with goal-setting. Broadly, cadets engage in the P-RAP process to document their short-, medium-, and long-term career goals, and to plan the steps required to meet these goals. Cadets work with program staff and their mentor(s) to establish and document their career goals using a template that walks cadets through the goal-setting process (Appendix A shows one example of a P-RAP template). Mentors are adults who are selected (in most cases by the cadet) to support the cadet with the development and documentation of their career goals. By design, they begin working with the cadet during the residential phase of the program and continue working with the cadet during the post-residential phase to facilitate their transition to their selected educational or career goal. Although all sites engage in the P-RAP process, some sites have made modifications to the P-RAP template and to the implementation/process to best fit their individual sites' needs and capacities.[1]

The way in which the P-RAP process is integrated into the ChalleNGe Program varies significantly across sites. All sites use the P-RAP template as a tool to support the process of identifying and documenting the goal-setting process, although the specific format and content vary across sites (Table C.1 illustrates common elements included in the P-RAP template across sites and gives a sense of the variation). Some sites have a formal P-RAP course in which cadets learn about goal-setting, college degrees and certificate programs, branches of the military, and various job sectors. For example, cadets might take a personal interest inventory, investigate career pathways, complete job applications, do mock interviews, participate in a career fair, and prepare resumes and cover letters. Upon completing the course, cadets might complete a P-RAP portfolio, which is the culmination of their work in the course. In at least one case, they present

---

[1] Programs are instructed to use the P-RAP beginning early in the residential period, to make sure the P-RAP is updated throughout the residential period, and to provide a copy to the mentor. Within these guidelines, the staff have control of the process and the template and can modify both as they see fit. Over time, staff have had the opportunity to share information on how they use the P-RAP (and on other aspects of program management) at twice-yearly conferences.

their P-RAP portfolio to the cadets in their platoon and ChalleNGe academy staff. During the presentation, the cadets receive feedback on their P-RAP portfolios.

At other sites, the cadets work individually in consultation with program staff to complete the P-RAP. Some programs have cadets work on the P-RAP every week, while others have cadets work on them every few weeks or just a few times during the course of the program. There were also differences in start times for working with the cadet on the P-RAP.

Rather than providing feedback on goals, staff at one of these sites indicated that they primarily provide feedback on sentence and paragraph structure because cadets "need to learn how to write" (ChalleNGe staff, verbal discussion with the authors, December 2018). At this site, they use goal cards in which cadets write very short-term (day-to-day) goals, e.g., "do 70 pushups" or "turn in my math assignment on time." Program staff indicated that the cadets find the goal cards to be useful. Interestingly, this site uses a written goal-setting template that asks cadets to set lifetime goals, followed by a 25-year plan of smaller goals that should be achieved if they are to reach their lifetime plan. Then they ask cadets to set five-year, one-year, six-month, and one-month goals related to the lifetime goals. Finally, they ask cadets to set a daily to-do list of things to do to achieve the lifetime goals. This stepwise process might be where the "goal cards" originated. Given the literature on reasonable time horizons for possible identities, setting a lifetime goal might not be effective.

To demonstrate the importance of identifying clear and specific steps required to achieve a goal, some sites use the "sandwich exercise" in which cadets give step-by-step instructions to the site's commandant on how to make a peanut butter and jelly sandwich. Despite the simplicity of the goal, it typically takes the cadets several rounds of instruction before they can state the steps with enough clarity and specificity and in the correct order that "the sandwich can be made."

Despite the high degree of variability in the implementation of the P-RAP, our findings revealed several key components that consistently emerge across sites and/or templates that we reviewed. Specifically, in our analysis we found that most sites engaged in the following themes when implementing the P-RAP process:

- exploration of opportunities
- identification of goals
- creation of an actionable plan
- documentation through the P-RAP template
- support from key adults
- youth engagement
- execution and follow-up during post-residential phase.

Next, we highlight findings related to these key themes of the P-RAP process.

Exploration of Opportunities

A prerequisite for setting goals is being aware of possibilities. The extent to which ChalleNGe sites provided opportunities for cadets to explore career opportunities varied significantly. At some sites, there are many opportunities to explore options. For example, some sites have vocational training programs in residence where cadets can learn a vocation, e.g., construction, masonry, carpentry, and firefighting. Some sites have P-RAP field trips where cadets visit an industry, a business, a technical college, a furniture store, a heavy equipment training center, etc. Some sites also do mock interviews, resume development, etc., to assist in getting the cadets workforce-ready. One site reported that a technical college puts on a "reality day" where cadets each draw a card and spend a day in the life of the person described on the card, e.g., unmarried, two kids, works at fast food restaurant, $800 per month income; single, office job, $2,500 per month income. All of these experiential activities are geared toward exposing the cadets to possibilities.

Other ChalleNGe sites offer opportunities to explore personal interests. For instance, one site has numerous clubs and activities held at lunchtime every day to allow cadets to explore potential areas of interest and talent, e.g., honor guard, run club, drumline, coding academy, collegiate cohort, nature club, drill team, yearbook club, music club, sculling club, student council, and game club. The staff at this site believe that cadets need to be exposed to a wide variety of activities to determine possible interests and talents. These clubs and activities are run by program staff. Although not directly related to career choice, these experiences might help the cadets develop personally meaningful goals (recall from the previous chapter that adolescents who develop personally meaningful goals are more likely to achieve those goals).

The Jobs ChalleNGe Program is a career and technical education program available at some sites for graduates of the ChalleNGe Program. It provides ChalleNGe graduates with education and job training programs that allow cadets to obtain a certificate in a vocational field, job shadow, intern, and ultimately obtain employment with local employers, e.g., in manufacturing, construction, the automotive industry, trades, or cyber-security. This type of program provides youth with extended behavioral involvement in the selected field, thus increasing an adolescent's chances of developing an identity related to a particular type of work.

Identification of Goals

The P-RAP is used to help cadets set appropriate goals so that they can be successful during and after the post-residential phase. Across all ChalleNGe sites, staff focus on placement (employment, education, or military) as the primary goal for the post-residential period. In support of this, several P-RAP templates have the following text at the beginning:

> Unless youth leave ChalleNGe with a realistic Post Residential Action Plan and the ability to continue to plan effectively throughout their lives, they are unable to maximize this second chance. To be successful, ChalleNGe youth must graduate from the program with a working plan, a functional skill set for planning, and guidance in Post Residential Action Plan implementation.

Although it is clear that placement is valued at all of the sites, the specific emphasis differs somewhat across sites. Most programs focus on a minimum of 25 hours per week in total or in a combination of education (high school or college), employment, or military as a successful placement. Programs may or may not consider part-time schooling (such as online programs), part-time work, or community service to be a successful placement.

Some programs consider active job-seeking as placement. Furthermore, the quality of employment does not necessarily indicate the success of the placement, especially if the cadet is also going to school at the same time. On the other hand, a director at one site stated,

> if we could make arrangements for all of our cadets to be placed at McDonald's or some other fast food restaurant, we would technically have 100 percent placement. But we are focused on more than just placement—we are focused on the cadets having a sustainable future (ChalleNGe site director, verbal discussion with the authors, September 2019).[2]

Regardless of whether the goal placement is school, employment, or military, program staff work with the cadets to determine what steps they need to take to achieve their placement goal. For example, interviewees indicated that for cadets planning to return to high school, program staff would determine what courses the cadet was missing and develop a plan around those courses. For cadets interested in joining the workforce, program staff would help them create resumes. For cadets interested in attending college, program staff might help cadets fill out applications and complete financial aid forms. For cadets interested in joining the military, program staff might help cadets coordinate with local recruiters. Some programs encourage cadets to include vocational training in their P-RAP.

Creation of an Actionable Plan

Almost universally across sites, the P-RAP process involves the creation of an actionable plan to attain cadets' goals. To support this process, the P-RAP templates include short-term, intermediate, and long-term goals. The short-term goals across sites focus on the eight core components of the ChalleNGe Program (academic excellence, health and hygiene, job skills, leadership

---

[2] To some extent, the specific placement goal is governed by age. For example, 16-year-old cadets might have a difficult time placing into higher education or the workforce upon graduation. Being younger is also typically indicative of less experience, which makes workforce placement more difficult.

and followership, life-coping skills, physical fitness, responsible citizenship, and service to community). One site encourages cadets to focus on setting short-term goals focused on personal performance, skills, or knowledge to be acquired (akin to learning-oriented goals), in contrast to goals based on outcomes (e.g., finishing in the top three in a race, akin to performance-oriented goals). Intermediate and long-term goals are all focused on placement, housing, and transportation. Some sites explicitly state that the transportation and housing goals should support the placement goal.

Across sites, the short-term goals focus on an end period of five months—while the cadets are in the residential phase of the program. Intermediate goals focus on the end of the 12-month post-residential phase. Although the time horizon of short-term and intermediate goals is similar across sites, the specified period for long-term goals varies across sites, with most ranging from two to five years postgraduation, but some with time horizons as long as ten to 15 years. The P-RAP templates with the longer time horizons ask the cadets to *"Think ahead to what life as an adult would look like for you. Describe an 'ideal' but realistic career, transportation and housing goal. Where do you want to be in 5 years? 10 years? 15 years?"*

In addition to specifying the time horizons, we found that most sites specify that goals must be written in SMART goal format. Although it is possible, perhaps even likely, that all sites require SMART goal format, not all P-RAP documents include this information. In addition, some templates provide tangible examples of SMART goals, e.g., "create a resume by week 15," "improve my math grade by two grade levels by week 21" for the cadets.

Finally, review of the P-RAP templates indicated that most sites ask cadets to outline the steps needed to achieve their goal(s), identify barriers or obstacles to achieving their goal(s), list strategies to overcome the barriers/obstacles, and describe resources that can be used to support them in achieving their goals. For four of the 15 sites, cadets also specify backup or alternate placement, housing, and transportation plans in the event that something happens that prevents them from achieving their primary goals. Seven of the 15 sites indicate that the cadet should specify transition/bridge plans for the period of time immediately following graduation and prior to starting a job, enrolling in school, or enlisting in the military. However, only three of the 15 sites ask the cadets to consider the relative advantages and disadvantages of their specified placement goals.

Documentation Through the P-RAP Template

All ChalleNGe sites use the P-RAP template to document the goal-setting process for cadets (see Table C.1). The format of the P-RAP template differs across sites, with some P-RAPs being fairly structured (e.g., New Mexico), while others are more open-ended (e.g., Montana). One of the most notable differences is that the P-RAP documents vary considerably in length across sites, ranging from one page to 50 pages (with an average length of about 12 pages). Most sites use a single P-RAP template; however, some do use separate forms for short-term, intermediate, and long-term goals. Some sites explicitly refer to the P-RAP as a "living document" that will grow and change as the cadet grows and changes, and as a "roadmap for success" in the post-residential phase of ChalleNGe. Also, some P-RAPs explicitly state that the plans should be created using the C-A-D-E-T success model (connect, analyze, decide, plan and execute, test) to connect the residential to the post-residential phase. Some sites ask the cadet to complete a day-by-day calendar in which they are to list a constructive and productive activity for each day of the month. Approximately half of the sites list deadlines (by date or week of residential program) to complete specific aspects of the P-RAP. Although it is possible, even likely, that the other sites also have deadlines, they are not specified in the templates themselves.

Support from Key Adults

According to feedback from our interviews with ChalleNGe staff, the P-RAP process depends heavily on the support from both ChalleNGe staff members and mentors. Program staff work with the cadets to determine what steps they need to take to achieve their placement goal. For example, ChalleNGe staff shared that for cadets planning to return to high school, program staff would determine what courses the cadet was missing and develop a plan around these courses. For cadets interested in joining the workforce, program staff could help them create resumes. For cadets interested in attending college, program staff might help cadets fill out applications and complete financial aid forms. For cadets interested in joining the military, program staff might help cadets coordinate with local recruiters.

Some programs encourage cadets to include vocational training in their P-RAP. At a minimum, most sites require P-RAP plans (i.e., the completed templates) be signed off/approved by the ChalleNGe academy staff.

However, the degree of involvement of staff varies across sites. For instance, the number of staff involved in P-RAP implementation differs across sites. At some sites, each cadet works with a designated staff team, e.g., counselor, teacher, and team leader. At other sites, a specific staff person is designated to work with all cadets and sign off on their P-RAPs. Additionally, the level of staff buy-in (i.e., the extent to which staff believe the P-RAP process is a priority and beneficial, and their openness to engage in the process) for the P-RAP among ChalleNGe staff differs across sites. It is clear that staff in some programs believe that the P-RAP is essential for long-term success. At two sites, program staff indicated that it is very common for staff to approach cadets and ask them about their P-RAP. In contrast, some staff at other sites believe the P-RAP is too long and too detailed for cadets at their current stage in life, and that it would be more effective to have "a life plan, a list of life goals or a list of specific careers." As a result, some programs use a modified version of the P-RAP or have cadets fill out supplementary placement forms.

In addition to ChalleNGe staff, mentors play a key role in supporting cadets as they develop their goals and create a plan for the post-residential phase. Mentors, who have been nominated by the cadets, are matched with cadets during the residential phase. Mentors help support the cadets during the latter portion of the residential phase and help them prepare to reenter community life. Mentors continue their responsibilities throughout the 12-month post-residential phase, also reporting cadet placement activities to the sites. Guidance indicates that mentors should be in regular contact with mentees (e.g., approximately two times a month, although more-frequent contact is encouraged). The ChalleNGe Program notes that mentors play a critical role in ensuring cadets' continued success, helping the youth transition from the structured environment of the residential phase to self-management and guiding them through the implementation of their life plans developed as part of the P-RAP process. Information from the interviews suggests that many sites lack mentors who are prepared to facilitate adherence to the P-RAP and that mentor contact often drops off sharply after the residential phase. These problems may have to do with how mentors are selected at some sites and/or the intensity of the contact. At one site, staff indicated that the mentors are selected by the cadets, who generally do not have good role models. At that site, the cadets are asked to write a postcard to their mentor once per week. Weekly postcards are not likely to be a sufficient mechanism for developing a meaningful relationship with a mentor. Another site reported that mentors could be a principal, teacher, a friend of the family, or a distant relative, but not a close family member (in some cases, sites apply for a waiver to designate a close family member as the mentor). That site reported better contact between cadets and mentors.

Youth Engagement

Programs recognize that cadets must actively participate in their P-RAP in order for it to be successful. Program staff guide cadets on the P-RAP and encourage them to take ownership of their future.

At one site, program staff described an important difference between *trust* buy-in and *value* buy-in among cadets. They described trust buy-in as cadets just getting through, enduring, and submitting, but not really seeing value in the P-RAP. For these cadets, the P-RAP is viewed as an assignment. They described value buy-in as cadets *internalizing the value* of the P-RAP. For these cadets, it is more than an exercise or assignment. ChalleNGe staff shared that they strongly believe that value buy-in is critical to cadet long-term success.

Program staff also reported that some cadets do not buy into the process at all: They fail to complete the P-RAP because they are just not interested. Program staff report that there is not much they can do with cadets such as these. The lack of interest in the P-RAP could reflect limited exposure to future possibilities or the lack of belief that change is possible for them. It is also not clear how much cadet buy-in might be influenced by staff buy-in and vice versa.

Execution and Follow-Up During Post-Residential Phase

The 12-month post-residential phase begins when graduates leave the ChalleNGe academy and return to their communities. Graduates return to high school, pursue higher education, find a job, join the military, or volunteer at least 25 hours a week as a placement. The goal of this phase is for graduates to sustain and build on the gains made during the residential phase, and to apply the new skills they have learned to their home environment. In addition, they are expected to continue to develop and implement their life plans from their P-RAP.

Most programs do not collect systematic, in-depth placement data that would enable them to track cadets' adherence to the P-RAP and better understand the usefulness of the process. Programs may know which graduates have reenrolled in high school, but they do not collect data on graduation rates. Programs may collect information on number of hours worked (to determine whether the hours worked constitute placement), but collect little data on wages, benefits, occupation, or turnover. Some programs, however, do keep track of whether graduates adhere to the P-RAP. According to one site, roughly 60 percent of cadets stay within the track indicated on the P-RAP.

Mentors are supposed to be the primary source of post-residential information, but reliability is low. During the post-residential year, mentors are tasked with monthly reports and noting whether the cadet has veered from the original P-RAP. Because contact with mentors drops precipitously during the post-residential phase, post-residential information is often verified through other methods; this means that program staff spend much time tracking down graduates and verifying employment using a variety of means, including pay stubs sent in by graduates, social media information (e.g., pictures of cadets in work uniforms on Facebook), and school transcripts.

There is considerable variation in rates of follow-up. For example, one site reported that they are in contact with only 20 percent of cadets six months after the program, while another site reported that they are in contact with 90 percent of cadets six months after the program. The complete set of factors that drive this variation is unclear, but staff roles in follow-ups may help to explain differential rates in follow-ups. One site reported that one reason they have a greater success rate with follow-ups than other sites is because counselors do the follow-up rather than recruitment, placement, and mentoring staff. They indicated that, because the cadets worked closely with counselors during the residential phase, cadets tend to be responsive to counselors during the follow-up period.

Key Takeaways

Review of the templates and interview notes from the sites highlighted several themes across sites regarding how the ChalleNGe Program implements the P-RAP process. Specifically, all sites integrate the following into the P-RAP process for their cadets:

- exploration of opportunities
- identification of goals
- creation of an actionable plan
- documentation through the P-RAP template
- support from key adults
- youth engagement
- execution and follow-up during post-residential phase.

That said, there is a considerable difference in the manner in which each of these themes is implemented and the overall perceived value of the P-RAP process across sites. The template itself offers some consistency across sites, with most utilizing SMART goals and providing structures to help cadets develop and document an actionable plan for the post-residential phase. However, characteristics such as format (length and detail of the template), time horizons for long-term plans, the focus of the goals, and the degree of involvement from staff and mentors varied from site to site. Additionally, staff at some sites believe that the P-RAP is critical whereas staff at other sites believe that the P-RAP is not particularly useful. These differences are evidenced in part by the amount of time dedicated to the P-RAP, the number of staff involved in the P-RAP, the level of staff buy-in, variety of opportunities presented, and cadet buy-in.

In the next chapter, we lay out the explicit connections between the relevant literature and the ways ChalleNGe sites use the P-RAP. Using these connections, we develop a series of recommendations.

CHAPTER FOUR

Lessons Learned and Recommendations

In this chapter, we reflect on our findings from the literature review, examination of the P-RAP template, and review of P-RAP implementation strategies across select sites to establish relevant lessons learned for the ChalleNGe Program. Drawing on these lessons learned, we provide high-level recommendations for how the ChalleNGe Program staff can improve the implementation process to best support the success of cadets across sites.

Lessons Learned

Research findings suggest a link between goal-setting and academic achievement, positive behavioral outcomes, and workforce readiness (e.g., Bruhn et al., 2016; Moeller, Theiler, and Wu, 2012; Schippers, Scheepers, and Peterson, 2015; Clements and Kamau, 2018). For youth who struggle with self-regulation and setting goals and who are at risk of dropping out of high school, early intervention to support effective goal-setting may be one mechanism for establishing a pathway to success. The ChalleNGe Program uses the P-RAP process to assist cadets in identifying highly personalized goals to support their transition from the academy to the post-residential phase and beyond.

P-RAP Is Well-Grounded in the Theoretical and Empirical Literature

The P-RAP is a well-designed process to assist youth in identifying highly personalized goals and developing action-oriented plans to support the transition to adult roles. As discussed in Chapter Two, the P-RAP templates appear to be derived from, or are at least consistent with, theoretical and empirical evidence about goal-setting in adolescents. Intermediate and long-term goals are appropriately focused on placement (work, school, or military), housing, and transportation—all essential for the successful transition to adulthood. Although the domains are specified, the cadets identify their own goals in each of these domains; thus, they are highly personalized. The P-RAP uses the SMART goal format; the goals are required to be clear and specific and include steps needed to achieve them and specific timelines.

Implementation of P-RAP Varies Across Sites

Although the design of the P-RAP is consistent with best practices identified in the literature, there is wide variation in how the P-RAP is used and implemented across sites (this is shown throughout Chapter Three). At some sites, the P-RAP is threaded throughout the entire program, and many, if not most, staff are involved in the P-RAP process. At these sites, the staff consider the P-RAP to be very valuable. At other sites, the P-RAP is viewed as more of an assignment to be completed so cadets can move on, and a single staff person is responsible for signing off on all of the cadet's P-RAPs. The staff at these sites indicated that they do not think the P-RAP is valuable. At some of the sites, the cadets present their P-RAP to their platoon and ChalleNGe staff for feedback prior to graduation. The staff believe this presentation leads the cadets to take ownership of the goals they laid out in their P-RAP. At some sites, there is greater opportunity for exploration of career options (e.g., Jobs ChalleNGe; exposure to local employers that will facilitate job shadowing and internship opportunities; education and training toward a certificate in a vocational program, etc.). Finally, at many sites, there is a lack of mentors who are prepared to work with the cadets on their P-RAP. Across sites, ChalleNGe staff report that mentor contacts drop off precipitously after the residential program. In the immediate post-residential phase, individual mentorship is likely essential to the cadet persisting in the pursuit of their placement goal (or goals).

Recommendations

Based on our review of the templates and interviews with site staff, the implementation of the P-RAP across sites often demonstrates alignment with findings from the literature. However, there are also areas of opportunity to improve the implementation process to best support success of the cadets. In this section, we align our findings from the literature review (Chapter Two) with our findings from our review of the sites (Chapter Three), providing recommendations on future use of the P-RAP across ChalleNGe sites. Although we recognize the need to allow for flexibility in the implementation of the P-RAP process across sites because of staff capacity and cadet needs, we recommend some basic practices that have the potential to benefit all sites.

Encourage Deeper and More Consistent Use of the P-RAP Across the Components of the ChalleNGe Program

Many aspects of the P-RAP process are well-aligned with the literature and some sites appear to implement the P-RAP process in a manner that is consistent with best practices. However, there is considerable variation in the ways that the P-RAP is implemented. The sites that weave the P-RAP through multiple aspects of the ChalleNGe Program come closer to the principles in the literature, and there is some evidence that this leads to greater success. In particular, both staff and cadets take more ownership of the process at these sites. To provide a specific example, the CICO program model uses regular and daily check-ins between students and a key school staff member to discuss progress toward goals (Hawken et al., 2014; Mitchell, Adamson, and McKenna, 2017). Feedback during interviews with select ChalleNGe sites suggested that those sites that engaged in more-frequent and ongoing touch-points had greater buy-in for the P-RAP process from both staff and cadets. Although daily check-ins may not be necessary given the longer-term purpose of the P-RAP, threading regular communication between cadets and staff throughout the residential phase has the potential to support goal identification and attainment and sends a clear message about its importance to the cadets' future success.

We recognize that site-level variation is a feature of the ChalleNGe Program, driven at least in part by the different environments in which sites operate; nonetheless, there appears to be room to increase consistency by encouraging some sites to weave the P-RAP more tightly into their program. The recommendations that follow offer specific ideas for sites seeking to better integrate the P-RAP process within their programs.

Ensure Adequate Exploration to Identify Meaningful Goals

Setting personally meaningful goals can facilitate the successful transition to adulthood. All three categories of placement goals (continued education, workforce, or military) are developmentally appropriate for the cadets (Erikson, 1968; Seiffge-Krenke, Kiuru, and Nurmi, 2010). But because goals must be personally meaningful to be motivating (Markus and Nurius, 1986; Nurra and Oyserman, 2018), the cadet must perceive the specific placement goal as important to whom they want to become, e.g., a *possible identity* as an electrician, teacher, or soldier. However, as noted in the literature, identifying one's career and academic goals may be more challenging for economically disadvantaged youth (De Haan and MacDermid, 1999; Hihara, Sugimura, and Syed, 2018; Phillips and Pittman, 2003). For this reason, providing multiple and ongoing experiences to let cadets learn about and explore their options would be beneficial. Some sites currently provide these types of in-depth exploration activities (e.g., offering vocational training programs in residence; partnering with a local technical college to conduct a "reality day"; and providing on-site clubs and activities so cadets can explore potential areas of interest and talent). These sites noted a high degree of both cadet and staff buy-in and engagement and might serve as models of promising practices for other sites that currently offer fewer opportunities.

Help Cadets Outline Goals That Are Specific, Challenging, and Attainable with Appropriate Time Metrics

Based on review of P-RAP templates and interviews with select sites, we found that several sites encourage this type of goal-setting among cadets through the use of the SMART goals framework. This generally involves using fine-grained time metrics for P-RAP goals. For instance, currently across sites, short-term goals focus on the eight core components of the program. Goals written with more–fine-grained time metrics (e.g., identify three methods to reduce stress by week three), may be more achievable than ones with longer time metrics (e.g., run one mile in less than 10 minutes on the weekly physical training test by graduation). Further consistency in the template formats or the approach for identifying short, intermediate, and long-term goals may enhance outcomes at sites where these practices are less strictly followed. Additionally, providing education to staff and mentors on the utility of the SMART goals framework, and providing cadets specific examples of SMART goals on the P-RAP templates, may offer a starting point to foster higher-quality goal-setting processes.

Incorporate Learning-Oriented Goals into the P-RAP

Although only one site reported encouraging learning-oriented goals (i.e., goals focused on personal performance, skills, or knowledge to be acquired), our review of the goal-setting literature suggests that incorporating the use of learning-oriented goals more consistently across sites may benefit cadets in the long run. Extensive research on learning versus performance-oriented goals (i.e., goals focused on external rewards or outperforming others) consistently finds that individuals who focus on learning-oriented versus performance goals are more likely to experience precursors of success, such as greater academic self-efficacy (Coutinho and Neuman, 2008; Phan, 2009), self-regulation (Hsieh et al., 2012), and academic achievement (Crippen et al., 2009; Hsieh, Sullivan, and Guerra, 2007; Phan, 2009). Encouraging cadets to focus on this type of goal, particularly for short-term goals, has the potential to establish an early foundation of success. Providing guidance to staff and mentors on how to foster learning-oriented goals (e.g., gaining knowledge for a particular trade) versus performance goals (e.g., getting the best grade in the class) and teach cadets the difference between these types of goals may help cadets develop more-useful and fulfilling goals during their time in the program.

Conclusion

Recognizing the importance of goal-setting in helping adolescents, particularly those at-risk for academic, social, or behavioral problems, establish a pathway to independence and success in adulthood, the ChalleNGe Program uses the P-RAP process to support cadets. Many aspects of the P-RAP process are well-grounded in goal-setting and adolescent development theory and empirical evidence. Therefore, the P-RAP may serve as a potential model for similar quasi-military programs—or other programs focused on at-risk youth—by demonstrating how to support career and academic goal-setting and attainment. That said, the manner in which ChalleNGe sites implement the P-RAP process appears to vary considerably; moving toward a more standardized approach has the potential to strengthen the program and thus to better prepare participants for long-term success.

Example of a P-RAP Template

The document reproduced here provides an example of a P-RAP template from the Wisconsin ChalleNGe Program.

Post-Residential Action Plan Worksheet

_____

(Print Full Name)

Complete the following steps using the S.M.A.R.T. Criteria for each goal and task.

Please use pencil!

STEP 1
My Long Term Goal
What is your vision of your life 2 to 5 years after graduation? What do you see yourself doing as a career or dream job?

STEP 2

Intermediate Placement Goal

You must choose one of the following options for your Intermediate Goal. This should be your primary goal for the 12 months after graduation, and support your Long-Term Goal

(Circle Your Choice)

EMPLOYMENT   EDUCATION   MILITARY   VOCATIONAL TRAINING

Write out your Intermediate Goal (be S.M.A.R.T.):

(Circle One)

Full-Time   Part-Time
(If you select *Part-Time*, you will need to enter a second part-time plan in Step 5)

List the expected start date for your Intermediate Goal

Date of graduation from the Challenge Academy is: _____

Start Date for Intermediate Goal is: _____

TASKS

Identify tasks you need to complete to reach your Intermediate Goal. Identify a deadline or a target date for completion and record in your planner.

Task:	Completion Date:
1.	_____
2.	_____
3.	_____
4.	_____
5.	_____

OBSTACLES

Identifying obstacles helps to prevent surprises that can occur in the future. Obstacles may cause us to change our plan or delay us from reaching our goal.

Identify obstacles that you will have to overcome to reach your goal (health, legal, financial, low test scores, living arrangements, lack of other resources). Also identify the tasks you need to complete to successfully overcome each obstacle.

Obstacle   **Task to Overcome Obstacle**

1.   1.

2.   2.

3.   3.

4.   4.

5.   5.

RESOURCES

List the resources you have available to help you complete the tasks and overcome the obstacles you have listed.

1.

2.

3.

4.

5.

STEP 3
Community Living Plan

Write out a living plan that supports your *Intermediate* Placement Goal.

TASKS

Identify tasks you need to accomplish for your plan to work. Identify a deadline or a target date for each one and record in your planner.

Task: **Completion Date:**

1.   _____

2.   _____

3.   _____

4.   _____

5.   _____

OBSTACLES

Identify obstacles you will have to overcome for your Community Living Plan, and identify the tasks you need to complete to successfully overcome each one.

Obstacle   **Task to Overcome Obstacle**

1.   1.

2.   2.

3.   3.

4.   4.

5.   5.

RESOURCES

List the resources you have available to help you complete the tasks and overcome the obstacles you have listed.

1.

2.

3.

4.

5.

STEP 4

Transportation Plan

Write out a transportation plan that supports your *Intermediate* Placement Goal.

TASKS

Identify tasks you need to accomplish for your plan to work. Identify a deadline or a target date for each one and record in your planner.

Task: **Completion Date:**

1.   _____

2.   _____

3.   _____

4.   _____

5.   _____

OBSTACLES

Identify obstacles that you will have to overcome for your Transportation plan and identify the tasks you need to complete to successfully overcome each one.

Obstacle   **Task to Overcome Obstacle**

1.   1.

2.   2.

3.   3.

4.   4.

5.   5.

RESOURCES

List the resources you have available to help you complete the tasks and overcome the obstacles you have listed.

1.

2.

3.

4.

5.

STEP 5

Bridge Plan / 2nd Part-Time Placement

Write out a Bridge Plan or 2nd Part-Time Placement plan that supports your Intermediate Placement Goal.

If you need to complete a Bridge Plan and a 2nd Part-Time Placement complete your 2nd Part-Time Placement here and ask your sponsor for another copy of Step 5 to complete your Bridge Plan.

TASKS

Identify tasks you need to accomplish for your plan to work. Identify a deadline or a target date for each one and record in your planner.

Task: **Completion Date:**

1.   _____

2.   _____

3.   _____

4.   _____

5.   _____

OBSTACLES

Identify obstacles that you will have to overcome for your plan, and identify the tasks you need to complete to successfully overcome each one.

Obstacle   **Task to Overcome Obstacle**

1.   1.

2.   2.

3.   3.

4.   4.

5.   5.

RESOURCES

List the resources you have available to help you complete the tasks and overcome the obstacles you have listed.

1.

2.

3.

4.

5.

Site Visit Protocols

In this appendix, we describe relevant protocols. In the course of this research, we examined notes from a series of earlier site visits and also carried out targeted site visits to learn more about how sites use the P-RAP.

The protocols from the earlier site visits covered a relatively wide array of topics, including questions focused on the program's core mission, opportunities and challenges, recruiting strategies, resources, staffing, community relations, and cadet placement (employment, education, military enlistment, etc.) after leaving ChalleNGe. Finally, the protocol included several questions on measuring and tracking program completion and success. The questions focused on P-RAP were included in the section on cadet placement; these questions are reproduced on the next page.

Placement/Life after ChalleNGe:

Preparing for placement:

- Do you use the P-RAP (Post-Residential Action Plan)? Have you modified the P-RAP in any way?
  - Do you find the P-RAP to be effective?
- Could you please describe your methods for working with cadets to complete the P-RAP?

Placement:

- How do you approach placement? What constitutes a successful placement? What prevents graduates from attaining successful placements?
  - Do you collect any information on the extent to which cadets follow their P-RAPs or other plans?

During the targeted site visits, we again held a series of semi-structured conversations; our protocol included the following questions:

- Please describe how the P-RAP is implemented at your site
  - At what point is the P-RAP introduced to the cadets?
  - Which staff member(s) introduce the P-RAP to the cadets?
  - How often does the cadet work on the P-RAP?

- Is there a formal course (focused on completing the P-RAP) or is the P-RAP completed independently?
  - Who reviews the P-RAP? When do they review it?
  - Do the cadets present their P-RAP? If so, to whom?
  - When is the P-RAP considered "complete?"

Prior to the end of the visit, we made sure to obtain copy of P-RAP document(s).

Elements Included in the P-RAP Template

In this appendix, Table C.1 illustrates common elements included in the P-RAP template across sites and gives a sense of the variation among programs.

TABLE C.1

Comparison of Elements Included in the P-RAP Template Across Sites

Site	Total Pages	Definition of SMART Goals	Example Goals	Detailed Steps to Achieve Goal	Barriers and Actions to Overcome Barriers	Resources Needed	Backup or Alternate Plan	Transition or Bridge Plan
California (Stockton)	1	—	—	—	—	—	—	—
Hawaii	50	X	—	X	X	X	—	X
Idaho	12	X	—	X	X	X	—	—
Illinois	12	X	X	X	X	X	—	—
Indiana	19	X	—	X	X	X	X	X
Kentucky	25	X	X	—	—	—	—	—
Michigan	12	X	—	X	X	X	X	—
Montana	8	—	—	—	—	—	X	—
New Jersey	26	X	—	X	X	X	—	X
New Mexico	20	X	X	X	X	X	X	X
Oregon	20	—	—	X	X	X	—	X
Virginia	12	X	—	X	X	X	—	—
West Virginia	4	X	X	X	X	X	—	—
Wisconsin	9	—	—	X	X	X	X	—
Wyoming	17	X	X	X	X	X	—	X

NOTE: — indicates element was not present in the site's P-RAP document; X indicates element was present in the site's P-RAP document.

Abbreviations

C-A-D-E-T	connect, analyze, decide, plan and execute, test
ChalleNGe	National Guard Youth Challenge
CICO	Check-In/Check-Out
P-RAP	Post-Residential Action Plan
SMART	specific, measurable, attainable, realistic, time-bound

References

Aghera, A., M. Emery, R. Bounds, C. Bush, R. B. Stansfield, B. Gillett, and S. A. Santen, "A Randomized Trial of SMART Goal Enhanced Debriefing After Simulation to Promote Educational Actions," *Western Journal of Emergency Medicine*, Vol. 19, No. 1, 2017, pp. 112–120.

Austin, J. T., and J. B. Vancouver, "Goal Constructs in Psychology: Structure, Process, and Content," *Psychological Bulletin*, Vol. 120, No. 3, 1996, pp. 338–375.

Barbrack, C. R., and C. A. Maher, "Effects of Involving Conduct Problem Adolescents in the Setting of Counseling Goals," *Child and Family Behavior Therapy*, Vol. 6, No. 2, 1984, pp. 33–43.

Bruhn, A. L., S. C. McDaniel, J. Fernando, and L. Troughton, "Goal-Setting Interventions for Students with Behavior Problems: A Systematic Review," *Behavioral Disorders*, Vol. 41, No. 2, 2016, pp. 107–121.

Clark, L. F., K. S. Miller, S. S. Nagy, J. Avery, D. L. Roth, N. Liddon, and S. Mukherjee, "Adult Identity Mentoring: Reducing Sexual Risk for African-American Seventh Grade Students," *Journal of Adolescent Health*, Vol. 37, No. 4, 2005, pp. 337.e1–337.e10.

Clements, A. J., and C. Kamau, "Understanding Students' Motivation Towards Proactive Career Behaviours Through Goal-Setting Theory and the Job Demands–Resources Model," *Studies in Higher Education*, Vol. 43, No. 12, 2018, pp. 2279–2293.

Constant, Louay, Jennie W. Wenger, Linda Cottrell, Wing Yi Chan, and Kathryn Edwards, *National Guard Youth ChalleNGe: Program Progress in 2017–2018*, Santa Monica, Calif.: RAND Corporation, RR-2907-OSD, 2019. As of August 20, 2021:
https://www.rand.org/pubs/research_reports/RR2907.html

Corte, C., and R. A. Zucker, "Self-Concept Disturbances: Cognitive Vulnerability for Early Drinking and Early Drunkenness in Adolescents at High Risk for Alcohol Problems," *Addictive Behaviors*, Vol. 33, No. 10, 2008, pp. 1282–1290.

Coutinho, S. A., and G. Neuman, "A Model of Metacognition, Achievement Goal Orientation, Learning Style and Self-Efficacy," *Learning Environments Research*, Vol. 11, No. 2, 2008, pp. 131–151.

Crippen, K. J., K. D. Biesinger, K. R. Muis, and M. Orgill, "The Role of Goal Orientation and Self-Efficacy in Learning from Web-Based Worked Examples," *Journal of Interactive Learning Research*, Vol. 20, No. 4, 2009, pp. 385–403.

De Haan, L. G., and S. M. MacDermid, "Identity Development as a Mediating Factor Between Urban Poverty and Behavioral Outcomes for Junior High School Students," *Journal of Family and Economic Issues*, Vol. 20, June 1999, pp. 123–148.

Drucker, P. F., *The Practice of Management*, New York: Harper & Row, 1954.

Duckworth, A. L., T. Kirby, A. Gollwitzer, and G. Oettingen, "From Fantasy to Action: Mental Contrasting with Implementation Intentions (MCII) Improves Academic Performance in Children," *Social Psychological and Personality Science*, Vol. 4, No. 6, November 2013, pp. 745–753.

Dweck, C. S., "Motivational Processes Affecting Learning," *American Psychologist*, Vol. 41, No. 10, 1986, pp. 1040–1048.

Dweck, C. S., and E. L. Leggett, "A Social-Cognitive Approach to Motivation and Personality," *Psychological Review*, Vol. 95, No. 2, 1988, pp. 256–273.

Eby, L. T., T. D. Allen, S. C. Evans, T. Ng, and D. DuBois, "Does Mentoring Matter? A Multidisciplinary Meta-Analysis Comparing Mentored and Non-Mentored Individuals," *Journal of Vocational Behavior*, Vol. 72, No. 2, April 2008, pp. 254–267.

Elliott, E. S., and C. S. Dweck, "Goals: An Approach to Motivation and Achievement," *Journal of Personality and Social Psychology*, Vol. 54, No. 1, 1988, pp. 5–12.

Engle, P. L., and M. M. Black, "The Effect of Poverty on Child Development and Educational Outcomes," *Annals of the New York Academy of Sciences*, Vol. 1136, No. 1, June 2008, pp. 243–256.

Erikson, E. H., "Adolescence," in *Identity: Youth and Crisis*, New York: W. W. Norton and Company, Inc., 1968, pp. 128–135.

Evans, G. W., and P. Kim, "Childhood Poverty, Chronic Stress, Self-Regulation, and Coping," *Child Development Perspectives*, Vol. 7, No. 1, March 2013, pp. 43–48.

Farley, J. P., and J. Kim-Spoon, "Parenting and Adolescent Self-Regulation Mediate Between Family and Socioeconomic Status and Adolescent Adjustment," *Journal of Early Adolescence*, Vol. 37, No. 4, April 2018, pp. 502–524.

Flouri, E., and C. Panourgia, "Negative Automatic Thoughts and Emotional and Behavioural Problems in Adolescence," *Child and Adolescent Mental Health*, Vol. 19, No. 1, 2014, pp. 46–51.

Gong, X., C. Chen, and M. K. O. Lee, "What Drives Problematic Online Gaming? The Role of IT Identity, Maladaptive Cognitions, and Maladaptive Emotions," *Computers in Human Behavior*, Vol. 110, September 2020, pp. 1–14.

Hawken, L. S., K. Bundock, K. Kladis, B. O'Keeffe, and C. A. Barret, "Systematic Review of the Check-In, Check-Out Intervention for Students at Risk for Emotional and Behavioral Disorders," *Education and Treatment of Children*, Vol. 37, No. 4, 2014, pp. 635–658.

Hihara, S., K. Sugimura, and M. Syed, "Forming a Negative Identity in Contemporary Society: Shedding Light on the Most Problematic Identity Resolution," *Identity: An International Journal of Theory and Research*, Vol. 18, No. 4, 2018, pp. 325–333.

Hill, D., and D. Brown, "Supporting Inclusion of At Risk Students in Secondary School Through Positive Behaviour Support," *International Journal of Inclusive Education*, Vol. 17, 2013, pp. 868–881.

Hoyle, R. H., and M. R. Sherrill, "Future Orientation in the Self-System: Possible Selves, Self-Regulation, and Behavior," *Journal of Personality*, Vol. 74, No. 6, December 2006, pp. 1673–1696.

Hsieh, P.-H., J. R. Sullivan, and N. S. Guerra, "A Closer Look at College Students: Self-Efficacy and Goal Orientation," *Journal of Advanced Academics*, Vol. 18, No. 3, 2007, pp. 454–476.

Hsieh, P.-H., J. R. Sullivan, D. A. Sass, and N. S. Guerra, "Undergraduate Engineering Students' Beliefs, Coping Strategies, and Academic Performance: An Evaluation of Theoretical Models," *Journal of Experimental Education*, Vol. 80, No. 2, 2012, pp. 196–218.

Latham, G. P., and E. A. Locke, "New Developments in and Directions for Goal-Setting Research," *European Psychologist*, Vol. 12, No. 4, 2007, pp. 290–300.

Lee, C.-K., C. Corte, K. F. Stein, C. G. Park, L. Finnegan, and L. L. McCreary, "Prospective Effects of Possible Selves on Alcohol Consumption in Adolescents," *Research in Nursing & Health*, Vol. 38, No. 1, February 2015, pp. 71–81.

Lewis, N. A., Jr., and D. Oyserman, "When Does the Future Begin? Time Metrics Matter, Connecting Present and Future Selves," *Psychological Science*, Vol. 26, No. 6, April 2015, pp. 816–825.

Locke, E. A., and G. P. Latham, *A Theory of Goal-Setting and Performance*, Englewood Cliffs, N.J.: Prentice-Hall, Inc., 1990.

———, "Building a Practically Useful Theory of Goal Setting and Task Motivation: A 35-Year Odyssey," *American Psychologist*, Vol. 57, No. 9, September 2002, pp. 705–717.

———, "New Directions in Goal-Setting Theory," *Current Directions in Psychological Science*, Vol. 15, No. 5, October 2006, pp. 265–268.

Locke, E. A., K. G. Smith, M. Erez, D.-O. Chah, and A. Schaffer, "The Effects of Intra-Individual Goal Conflict on Performance," *Journal of Management*, Vol. 20, No. 1, 1994, pp. 67–91.

Maher, C. A., "Effects of Involving Conduct Problem Adolescents in Goal Setting: An Exploratory Investigation," *Psychology in the Schools*, Vol. 18, No. 4, 1981, pp. 471–474.

Markus, H., and P. Nurius, "Possible Selves," *American Psychologist*, Vol. 41, No. 9, 1986, pp. 954–969.

Mitchell, B. S., R. Adamson, and J. W. McKenna, "Curbing Our Enthusiasm: An Analysis of the Check-In/Check-Out Literature Using the Council for Exceptional Children's Evidence-Based Practice Standards," *Behavior Modification*, Vol. 41, No. 3, May 2017, pp. 343–367.

Moeller, A. J., J. M. Theiler, and C. Wu, "Goal Setting and Student Achievement: A Longitudinal Study," *Modern Language Journal*, Vol. 96, No. 2, 2012, pp. 153–169.

Murru, E. C., and K. A. Martin Ginis, "Imagining the Possibilities: The Effects of a Possible Selves Intervention on Self-Regulatory Efficacy and Exercise Behavior," *Journal of Sport & Exercise Psychology*, Vol. 32, No. 4, 2010, pp. 537–554.

National Guard Youth ChalleNGe, *2015 Performance and Accountability Highlights*, Arlington, Va.: National Guard Bureau, 2015.

Nicholls, J. G., "Achievement Motivation: Conceptions of Ability, Subjective Experience, Task Choice, and Performance," *Psychological Review*, Vol. 91, No. 3, 1984, pp. 328–346.

Nurra, C., and D. Oyserman, "From Future Self to Current Action: An Identity-Based Motivation Perspective," *Self and Identity*, Vol. 17, No. 3, 2018, pp. 343–364.

Ouellette, J. A., R. Hessling, F. X. Gibbons, M. Reis-Bergan, and M. Gerrard, "Using Images to Increase Exercise Behavior: Prototypes Versus Possible Selves," *Personality and Social Psychology Bulletin*, Vol. 31, No. 5, May 2005, pp. 610–620.

Oyserman, D., K. Terry, and D. Bybee, "A Possible Selves Intervention to Enhance School Involvement," *Journal of Adolescence*, Vol. 25, No. 3, June 2002, pp. 313–326.

Phan, H. P., "Relations Between Goals, Self-Efficacy, Critical Thinking and Deep Processing Strategies: A Path Analysis," *Educational Psychology*, Vol. 29, No. 7, November 2009, pp. 777–799.

Phillips, T. M., and J. F. Pittman, "Identity Processes in Poor Adolescents: Exploring the Linkages Between Economic Disadvantage and the Primary Task of Adolescence," *Identity: An International Journal of Theory and Research*, Vol. 3, No. 2, 2003, pp. 115–129.

Pintrich, P. R., and D. H. Schunk, *Motivation in Education: Theory, Research, and Applications*, Englewood Cliffs, N.J.: Merrill, 1996.

Schippers, M., A. W. A. Scheepers, and J. B. Peterson, "A Scalable Goal-Setting Intervention Closes Both the Gender and Ethnic Minority Achievement Gap," *Palgrave Communications*, Vol. 1, 2015, pp. 1–12.

Schunk, D. H., "Goal Setting and Self-Efficacy During Self-Regulated Learning," *Educational Psychologist*, Vol. 25, No. 1, 1990, pp. 71–86.

Seiffge-Krenke, I., N. Kiuru, and J.-E. Nurmi, "Adolescents as 'Producers of Their Own Development'": Correlates and Consequences of the Importance and Attainment of Developmental Tasks," *European Journal of Developmental Psychology*, Vol. 7, No. 4, 2010, pp. 479–510.

Seijts, G. H., and G. P. Latham, "The Effect of Commitment to a Learning Goal, Self-Efficacy, and the Interaction Between Learning Goal Difficulty and Commitment on Performance in a Business Simulation," *Human Performance*, Vol. 24, No. 3, 2011, pp. 189–204.

Stein, K. F., R. Roeser, and H. R. Markus, "Self-Schemas and Possible Selves as Predictors and Outcomes of Risky Behaviors in Adolescents," *Nursing Research*, Vol. 47, No. 2, 1998, pp. 96–106.

Strachan, S. M., M. M. E. Marcotte, T. M. T. Giller, J. Brunet, and B. J. I. Schellenberg, "An Online Intervention to Increase Physical Activity: Self-Regulatory Possible Selves and the Moderating Role of Task Self-Efficacy," *Psychology of Sport and Exercise*, Vol. 31, 2017, pp. 158–165.

Wenger, Jennie W., Stephani L. Wrabel, Thomas E. Trail, Louay Constant, Wing Yi Chan, Kathryn A. Edwards, Joy S. Moini, and Hanna Han, *Developing Outcome Measures for the National Guard Youth Challenge (ChalleNGe) Program*, Santa Monica, Calif.: RAND Corporation, RR-A271-5, forthcoming.

Zhu, S., S. Tse, S.-H. Cheung, and D. Oyserman, "Will I Get There? Effects of Parental Support on Children's Possible Selves," *British Journal of Educational Psychology*, Vol. 84, No. 3, 2014, pp. 435–453.